NIGHTSCAPE

First published 2018 by Boxtree
an imprint of Pan Macmillan
20 New Wharf Road, London N1 9RR
Associated companies throughout the world
www.panmacmillan.com

ISBN 978-0-7522-6661-9

1 3 5 7 9 8 6 4 2

A CIP catalogue record for this book is available from the British Library.

Design by James Edgar Design
Typeset in Helvetica Neue

Printed and bound in China

Visit **www.panmacmillan.com** to read more about all our books
and to buy them. You will also find features, author interviews and
news of any author events, and you can sign up for e-newsletters
so that you're always first to hear about our new releases.

NIGHTSCAPE

NO LIMITS

BOXTREE

Contents

Introduction

Before the craziness begins — 6

Top of the world — 8

G

Ground Level – Starting Out

In the beginning — 14

Risk — 18

Fail, get up, fail harder — 24

Avoid comfort zones — 27

Dancing with the concrete — 30

Expand your possibilities — 33

Luck — 39

The city is a playground — 40

1

Rooftops – Finding My Way

Getting higher — 47

Find something you love more than sleep — 50

Why art? — 53

No rehearsals — 58

In love with the city — 60

Don't be ashamed of passion — 65

Fear — 66

Respect — 69

Life in the penthouse — 74

2

Rooftops – Spreading My Wings

Up in the clouds — 82

Perspective — 86

Outlaws — 93

Believe — 94

Opinions — 98

Your passion might not be someone else's — 103

Balfron Tower — 104

Petticoat Tower — 108

A bridge, Stratford — 111

Residential building, Elephant and Castle — 112

Barbican Estate — 116

3

Skyscrapers

The City within the city	122
Rebels	132
London Stadium	134
The Sidemen Tower	136
Humber Bridge	139
One Canada Square	140

4

Seeing
the World

Jakarta	146
Santorini	149
Make it challenging	152
Dubai	158
Shanghai	164

5

Behind
the Scenes

Kit	180
Editing	185
What's next?	186

Before the craziness begins

▶ Before we start, I want to be totally clear. I'm not interested in telling people what they should or shouldn't do, but this is really important: DO NOT READ THIS BOOK AND CLIMB UP BUILDINGS.
Climbing up buildings is hard. I've been training myself for more than ten years, so the risk makes sense for me, but only because of all that training. If I'd done less, I wouldn't be able to do the stuff you see in this book and be safe.

Bottom line: if you haven't learned to swim, you shouldn't just jump in the sea. If you can't drive, don't get behind the wheel of a Porsche. If you don't know exactly what your body is capable of, don't suddenly find out when you're 30 metres up in the air. I want you to read this book and see the world through my eyes, but that's very different to doing it yourself.

What I do want you to realize is that there are no limits to what you're capable of. That getting out in the world, using it in the way that you want to use it, not letting other people tell you which route to take, is what life is about. I want you to see that passion, dedication, not being afraid to try, not being afraid to fail, not being afraid to care deeply about what you do, are the things that matter. If someone tells me their life is boring, I know they just haven't found the thing that they love yet. No one ever said on their deathbed that they wished they'd done less. What stops us is fear. And I know a lot about overcoming fear. What I've realized is that climbing buildings is just a certain sort of problem. In life, it's how you solve problems that matters, and I want to show you how I do that.

Find your own passion. Climbing the city is mine but the world is filled with endless possibilities.

Top
of the
world

▶ I'm 200 metres high, on a crane in the centre of London, next to an almost-finished building shaped like a scalpel. It had been a while since I had done a decent climb, so I went out to find a viewpoint I could see the entire skyline from. The tallest thing I could see was this crane. I started the climb at 4 a.m. and now, two hours later, the first orange shades of the sunrise are just beginning to spread over the horizon.

After jumping the fence, and finding a route past the cameras and motion sensors to the bottom of the crane, it was pretty much ladders the whole way up, up to the control room and then finally along the 45-degree crane arm, the world narrowing to your hand reaching for each hold, your foot finding the next rung. I feel calm, there are no rash decisions. I concentrate on breathing slowly, making sure there are three points of contact. I am 100 per cent in control.

The crane sways back and forth in the wind. You can tell yourself they're designed to do that all you want, but believe me, you still forget it every single time it happens.

So, 200 metres – about three-quarters of the height of One Canada Square at Canary Wharf, or four Nelson's Columns. Not the highest I've been, but a pretty breathtaking view.

This part of London – skyscraper square – is where the new buildings have crazy names like the Gherkin, the Cheesegrater, the Walkie Talkie, the Shard and now the Scalpel. But in the distance I can see St Paul's, too, and the Bank of England, then the other way along the river there's Tower Bridge and the Tower of London. All these contrasting parts of the city that have grown up tangled together; all these people over hundreds of years, living and working and building lives, and I'm looking down on it, seeing it from a perspective that barely anyone ever gets to. I take photos because I want to document that, to share that experience, that emotion, with people.

The first traffic is just starting down below, but it's distant. It's so calm. Looking down, there's the whole of the horizon in front of me, the sun glinting on the glass and metal and the water. When you're at street level, the traffic noise is individual things – cars, motorbikes, sirens – but when you rise up above it, it all seems to blend together to create a background hum, a calming white noise created by a city that never stops.

There are plenty of people who would tell you I shouldn't be here, on this crane as the city wakes up beneath me. But right now, I can't think of anywhere I'd rather be.

Ground Level – Starting Out

In the beginning

Risk

Fail, get up, fail harder

Avoid comfort zones

Dancing with the concrete

Expand your possibilities

Luck

The city is a playground

In the beginning

▶ I used to be afraid of heights as a kid. Nobody believes that, but it's true. When people tell me that watching my videos or looking at the photos freaks them out, I get it. It's normal to be afraid of heights. It's a natural human instinct. You make a bad decision at ground level, that's one thing; you make a bad decision above about 5 metres and it's a whole different level of trouble. It's in our nature to be scared of heights; people in the past who weren't didn't last long. The trick is to overcome your fears, not ignore them.

I was an energetic kid. Even now I keep fidgeting, I can't keep still. My mum says I was always upside down on the sofa or climbing a tree. My parents had to find something for me to channel my energy into. I was always getting into trouble at school, always getting up to mischief.

I'd done gymnastics since I was about seven. I loved it. From the age of nine until about eleven I was training five days a week in the elite squad, training for the Olympics. It was expensive, but my mum and dad found a way.

Around that time my mum got sick. Stage 4 non-Hodgkin lymphoma. I didn't really understand what was going on, I didn't even know what cancer was, but as I got older I realized that it can happen to any one of us. You can keep your head down, avoid doing anything dangerous and this thing can still just reach into your life and change it forever.

After my mum got sick, I just didn't really like being told what to do anymore. Gymnastics is all about regular training, discipline and routine, and in the end the pressure got too much. I didn't want to do it; not when it meant long hours of training away from home. My mum knew I wasn't motivated to do it anymore, so even though she didn't understand how I could turn my back on potentially going to the Olympics, she let me stop going to training. It was about that time that I started getting into Parkour.

Risk

▶ What happened with my mum is one reason why I don't really agree when some people say it's selfish to put my loved ones through the worry of me doing what I do. The logical end result of that is that you wouldn't risk anything. Anything we have that is worth anything comes with the risk of it being taken from us.

If you really wanted to avoid risk, you'd stay inside, you'd never meet anyone, never make friends, never fall in love, because then you risk the sadness of losing them. I don't think it's selfish to do the thing that I love, that I'm passionate about, because I minimize the risk through training. Sometimes when I'm doing a video someone will stop me in the street and tell me that what I do is dangerous, and I say 'gymnastics is dangerous if you don't know what you're doing'. Honestly, some of the stuff I was doing as a kid was far more dangerous, it's just that you trust someone is taught how to do it. You try just rocking up with no training and doing a backflip. Have you seen the statistics on kids getting injured from rugby, or adults who hurt themselves going running? And don't even think about cycling in London.

Life is made of choices where you balance out what you're risking with what the reward is. My reward is seeing the world in a way that nobody else does. When you do something like that, when you're rewarded for pushing yourself, there's no better feeling in the world. I get it, though, people look at us and they see unskilled kids risking their lives for no reason. Whereas we see ourselves as highly skilled, in control of the risks and willing to make that trade because we're doing something we love.

►► My mum was incredibly strong through her
illness and got better. Of course, we've had
massive rows about my risky hobby in the past.
We still do from time to time. It's the first thing
that people ask: what does your mum think?
She'd probably say she's proud of me, but would
still rather I was obsessed with something else.
But my mum thinks it's amazing that there are
these people who feel strongly about what I do.
She reads comments from people saying that
watching my videos inspires them, gets emails
from mums saying their kids have started Parkour
because of me and they get out of bed to go train
in a Parkour gym and they're thanking me for
being part of that change in their lives. She gets
emotional about that.

What I do know is that the effort I put into my
skill set, the care I take to keep myself in the shape
I need to be, is huge compared to some bloke
sitting in a van smoking and texting as he drives.
There is nothing casual or careless about what
we do.

I'll be on a wall on a building in central London
and someone will come up to me and say 'What
are you doing? You could die!' And I always say,
I could die crossing the street, or riding a bike.
I'm far more aware, far more conscious of the risks
that I take and why I take them than 99 per cent
of people. You can spend your life trying to avoid
doing things that are dangerous and you could still
get sick. I'd rather look the danger in my life in the
eye and meet it head on. I'd rather back myself
and what I'm capable of. I trust my body more than
anything else. I could never get into skateboarding
or BMXing because that means putting my trust
in another object. With what I do, it comes down
to me trusting my body, my knowledge and my
experience. I train so I can do a jump at a couple
of metres from the ground and I know I can make
it 100 per cent of the time, then I make that jump
at 60 metres up. The only difference is mental.

Fail, get up, fail harder

► At around the time I stopped being into gymnastics, I remember I was in my living room watching a documentary called *Jump Britain*, which was the first time I ever saw freerunning. I remember sitting watching it, not being able to believe it was a thing. My brother and I spent the whole evening literally climbing up the walls, wedging ourselves in doorframes and swinging off window ledges. It wasn't just me – so many freerunners of my generation that I talk to got into it through this documentary.

Parkour is a discipline, like jiu-jitsu or kung fu. You learn it over time. It's about learning what your body's capabilities are. After years of training, I've got to a stage now where I know exactly how far I can jump, what my reach is, how my grip is going to hold out down to really precise amounts, even millimetres. There are lots of different moves with all sorts of names but really it's just about getting over any obstacle you could face.

Parkour started in these poor housing estates in France; the people living there didn't have wide open spaces or parks, or equipment to play sport, they just had their bodies and what was around them. It's why the sport is linked to hip hop and grime music now, because you're taking what you've got, even though it might not be much, and you're making something out of it.

You take these movements and you drill them again and again. You drill them until it becomes muscle memory and you can flow with your environment in a way that looks effortless. If you fail, you get back up and try again. You do this so many times that you begin to realize that failure is the learning process.

Anything I've ever done right, I've failed at a thousand times first. That's part of the process. Every success has been built on the foundations of failure. That's why freerunners see the world in a certain way. We become accustomed to pushing through mental challenges. Freerunning taught me how to take obstacles and failure and turn them into an opportunity to show my skills and passion. Everything I do in my life, every situation I approach is with this mindset. You stick a wall in my way, I'll find a way to jump over it. Every time I fail, I know it's one more step on that path to success, and every time something goes right, I don't lose my appreciation for failure.

Avoid comfort zones

▶ Anyone who dedicates themselves to any kind of training knows you can't progress in your comfort zone. Your muscles only grow if you force them to go beyond what they're currently capable of, and you should apply the same principle to your life. When you're in a comfort zone you're cruising. The moment you leave it, you'll start to see progress. You will be experiencing and learning new things, slowly becoming comfortable with things that once felt alien. Greatness isn't about doing better than other people, it's about constantly challenging yourself to be better than you were before.

But you have to be able to challenge yourself. That's not just in terms of risk and heights and that sort of physical stuff; I think people are afraid to commit, to feel, to admit that they care about things. People get trapped in this cycle of feeling negative, of everything being rubbish, of mocking everything, and that's just fear. Pretty much 99 per cent of the time, if someone's angry, or horrible, or takes the piss, that comes from a place of fear. If you can get free from that, find things that matter to you, admit things you care about, you feel fulfilled and happy.

The system that most of us live in is built to make you feel as if there's a void in your life that you need to fill. Because if you feel like that, you're easier to market to. They try and convince you that you can fill this void with material things – the latest Yeezy drop or a new car – that you can buy your way to happiness.

This surrounds us to such an extent that it feels as if there's nothing outside that system. In my twenty years on this planet, I've come to realize that the only things that actually give me a true sense of fulfilment aren't things I buy; rather, they are exploration and making art. Whether it's photography or videos, these are the things that help me feel free, and I'm sure it's the same for thousands of people out there.

Nothing compares to how I feel when I spend the whole day out exploring the city. There's nothing that anyone can sell me that makes me feel like that. The experiences I've had and the memories I've made with my best friends are priceless and will stick with me for the rest of my life. If you let yourself rely on things you buy to feel happy, if you let yourself be that predictable, you're not in charge of driving your own life, you're a passenger. You've got to find something – whether it's photography, sport, music, videos or writing – that's yours and that they can't get to.

I don't know why it is but the kind of people that I hang out with – freerunners, climbers, artists and YouTubers – all have this desire to create and channel our energy into our passions. We've all got some way of expressing ourselves – whether it's on a canvas or an Instagram feed. We've all got something that's ours.

Dancing with the concrete

► When we were starting out, we'd set ourselves these challenges, like we'd challenge each other to stick the jump, so you land it perfectly on your toes, without falling forwards or backwards. If you didn't stick it, you'd have to do ten push-ups. We'd practise our tech for hours, so that we knew we had the basics down before we started trying to do anything complicated. The London IMAX subway near Waterloo station is the home of London Parkour. I've spent so many hours there that it feels like my second home. We'd also go to the Southbank and train. We've spent years of our lives in total moving around that area. There's a thing within the London community about having the nicest technique. In London we have a really nice touch. Touch is when you land on your toes without making any noise. There's another subcategory of style called flow. This is about keeping your movements fluid as you move through the environment, making it feel as clean and effortlessly connected as possible. Spanish freerunners have this ability to incorporate flow into their movement. When you're doing it right there's this rhythm, this ease, it's like you're dancing with the concrete.

You have to be flexible, to see things from different angles and find the solution in the moment that works, that you're capable of doing. You have to be open and work with what you're given, not put pre-existing ideas onto a situation. My mum says it makes me a nightmare to argue with, because I've got an answer for everything. No matter what she says, I always try to see a different side, or try to change my approach as the argument goes on.

If everyone was taught, from a young age, how to interact with their environment in these ways, they would all have this natural physical ability. But also, freerunning is amazing for problem-solving, for thinking about how you're going to deal with the run in front of you.

And the thing is, it's fun. People do it naturally. Monkeys do it with their environment; kids do it when they're learning to walk – they pull themselves up on things, they crawl, they jump, they skip. At some point, we get taught not to do that, we ignore all these hundreds of thousands of years of running and jumping and climbing in the sun, playing with the world around us. We deny this bit of ourselves and we follow each other slowly through tunnels deep underground, and then we wonder why we feel sad.

Seriously, have you ever seen an unhappy person climbing a tree? You can't not smile.

Expand your possibilities

▶ Quite a few people message me asking how to get into freerunning and Parkour. My advice is that in most cities and big towns there will be a community. The easiest way is to look out for people training and start a conversation with them.

We're such a tight community and one of the friendliest set of open-minded people you could ever meet. The whole community is built on people helping each other get better at it. They'll want to talk, want to show you. If you feel like you don't want to start from zero in front of people, there are lots of videos online that will show you basic moves. There are indoor Parkour gyms around the country, where you can practise the basics in a controlled environment and there are instructors there too, who will be able to let you know the right places to look out for information in the local community. Go to events, go to jams, meet people, be friendly. Parkour has changed my life, opened up the way I see things. I owe everything I have to freerunning and the mindset that it's given me.

Luck

▶ Pretty much everything that's gone right for me has happened because of what looks like luck. If a cleaner hadn't left a mop and bucket wedged in the door in a part of West Ham's stadium we wouldn't usually have been able to get in, then that particular video wouldn't have blown up and got six million views in the way that it did and things might be very different now.

But the way I see it is that you have to put yourself in positions where luck can happen to you. You have to open yourself up to situations where timing and opportunity meet preparation, and when that comes together, this is what we perceive as luck. I honestly believe that if it hadn't been that video, it would have been another one, maybe later, but I would have put myself into positions that led to something happening.

The only way that you can guarantee you won't get the chance is if you never put yourself in the position in the first place.

You see this image on the left taken on a building next to the Shard? It's total chance that the bird is in the shot – that's what makes the image – but if I hadn't been there in the first place, no bird, no image.

Maximize your possibilities, take every opportunity you can. Life is about giving yourself the chance to be lucky.

The city is a playground

▶ After months and years of going out training, I started to see the city in a different way, and that was exciting. Where someone else sees a dark, gritty stairwell that stinks of piss, I see an opportunity to do something amazing. You start to use the space around you, as something you can be part of and that you can have a different sort of relationship with. In freerunning you can't dominate your surroundings – there's only going to be one winner between a human body and a concrete wall – you have to adapt yourself to whatever your surroundings provide. After a few years of training, you start to build a bond with the things around you, which is totally different to the way most people live in their city. They see it as ugly, covered in graffiti and litter. They find it hard to see the beauty hidden underneath. Another thing I've realized is that people in the city never look up. They never look around and see this amazing history and architecture right over their heads, that they walk past every day on their commute to work.

I think that's why the people who own the city feel so threatened by freerunning. There are all these rules and laws put in place for health and safety, and I'm sure some of that comes from a good place, but also it's a disobedient act to use the city how you want to, not how they tell you to. Once you start that, where does it end? You might decide you don't want to work all day in an office so you can afford to live in your over-priced rented flat and have your two-week holiday in the summer. You might stop buying the stuff they want you to buy.

I think the reason people get angry at us when they see us using the city as a playground is because there's a little bit of them that wishes they could too.

Rooftops –
Finding My Way

Getting higher

Find something you love more than sleep

Why art?

No rehearsals

In love with the city

Don't be ashamed of passion

Fear

Respect

Life in the penthouse

Getting higher

People see that you're in places you're not allowed to be without permission, but we see that there's so much beauty in these places and we want to experience it, capture it and document it so that other people can share in it. We weren't filming at first, just taking still photos. I wanted to capture the mad views that you get from the top of buildings. Me and my mates started meeting up, searching London, exploring all the time.

The photo on the next page is of where I grew up, taken near my mum's old house. With this, I wanted the contrast of the building and then nature. There's a tower block down the end of the road and it backs onto a massive forest. This is out towards Woodford. I lived opposite this park. To get this photo, I had to wedge my tripod out under a fence, away from the building, and balance it. Then I had to do a ten-second timer, press the button and run round to where I'd framed it. The silky clouds are one of my favourite aspects of this image, they're just like a photographer's dream.

Another time we were in the Barbican and we saw this thirty-storey building being renovated. We climbed up the scaffolding and went to the top of the building. We had to hide from the security guards. That was the first proper rooftop I did with two friends.

▶ For a little while, there started to be this bleed over from freerunning into exploring and climbing. It's like a natural overlap or progression; once you start to really use your surroundings in different ways, you start to think about going where people don't go at all, and in a city that naturally leads you to the top of buildings. We do it because we want to see the things that nobody else sees.

In the freerunning scene, training and film-making kind of go hand in hand. Growing up around these guys essentially meant I was surrounded by DSLRs and cameras used to film freerunning, and I knew I would do anything to own one myself. Being raised by a single mum, we didn't exactly have much disposable income. But I knew that getting my hands on one would give me endless possibilities. To save up, I took it upon myself to buy old Blackberrys and iPods from people at my school. I would repair them myself and then sell them on eBay. After a few months, I had an entire drawer filled with broken devices, but combined with Christmas and birthday money, I had enough cash to buy my first camera. I literally started off at the bottom – point and shoot – and moved my way up.

Rooftops – Finding My Way

50
51

Find something you love more than sleep

▶ I love this Millennium Bridge image because it's so literal – you can see the walkway and then you can see *our* walkway, almost like our own private pathway. I love the bruised-orange, early morning sky in this one, when the sun is just rising. Being up really early is amazing, because there's this whole other community of people – builders, street cleaners and office cleaners – coming home from work. So many different people and so many different mindsets. Often we'll be on a train at 8 a.m. coming back from a night of climbs, covered in building grime and mud, exhausted from a mad night, and all the morning commuters will be sitting opposite in their fresh suits on their way to work.

My mum probably thinks this is the most amazing thing about this stuff – that I'm up so early. Basically, for two years of my life I became partially nocturnal, sleeping all day and going out to explore and shoot at night. Now, as I've got more into it and the channel has taken off, I have way more responsibilities than I used to.

I feel like you could apply this as a life rule. Once you find something you're willing to leave the ultimate comfort zone of bed for, then you're on the right path. Find something you love more than sleep.

Why art?

▶ Some people start with doing the climb,
and videoing it or taking photographs of it is
secondary, it's just about documenting it.
There are people who are completely
underground, who document their adventures
but post nothing, and keep it on a drive at home.
Some post to private Instagram. Then there
are those that are in it for the views and the
clout. I don't blame them, everyone has their
hustle. I just wish they'd be more careful with
what they post and realize that every post,
every action has a reaction and consequences.
My intention has always been to make something
beautiful. It always will be. It has never been about
the social status. It doesn't matter to me how
many views I'm getting on YouTube, or how many
likes on Instagram. I do it because it's my passion.
You ask most guys my age, they want to make
something beautiful and they'd get embarrassed
because it's soft somehow, but I think that's
mad – don't let beauty be owned by other people.
It comes down to passion; if you're truly doing
it and enjoy it and it makes someone feel an
emotion, it will show. You can see when it's not
authentic; when someone's just doing it for the
status. You can tell.

►► I tell people I do it for the art. I think it's ridiculous that anyone would think art's not for them. It's one of the things in the world that can cause the most happiness. You want to have beauty in your life. Don't believe that people like you aren't allowed. How sad would it be if the only reason you keep away from beauty is because you're afraid of admitting that you feel? Men are so afraid of saying something's beautiful. You find anyone who's successful and you'll see that they've made that part of their lives. If you sit there laughing at the idea of things being beautiful, you're missing out on this massive thing. I used to be like that until I started appreciating the small things that people don't think are beautiful, like concrete stairwells. Then you start looking at things, you start finding photographers you like, looking at who they're influenced by. And you realize there's this whole world out there.

My photographs are all centred around making the viewer feel something – often that's shock or fear, but sometimes I want them to notice something beautiful. There are plenty of places where you can see people hanging from cranes or doing dangerous stuff, if that's what you're into, but it's not saying anything else. I try to make it about more than that. I want people to be inspired, to feel as though they too can make the decision to get out into the world and express themselves, regardless of what people think of them.

I want people to see the stuff I make and become part of that story – 99 per cent of people don't get to see the world from the perspectives that I do. And I think it's an angle that they should see the world from.

I'm far more interested in images that have a person in them, so you can see the relationship between the city and people. People seem to want the big landscapes with just buildings in them for posters, but I want the figures in there too.

You have to keep in mind that in the modern age of social media, imitation and attention-seeking has become a priority in people's lives. Many people do things that aren't true to their real selves for the sole purpose of attention and fame. I enjoy the attention and fame I get from my photos and videos and it's nice to be told that people enjoy what I do, but it's never been about the praise first. I love what I do, I care about editing, I care about creating films and telling stories. I have the desire to make everything not with the least effort I can get away with, but to the very best of my ability.

No
rehearsals

▶ So for a few years I was at school but all my
evenings and weekends I was just out
freerunning, climbing, getting shots. Teachers
would ask me what I wanted to do when I left
school and I'd say be a freerunner, and they'd
look at me like I was crazy. My family thought
I'd grow out of it and settle down, so when
I left school I tried a few different jobs.
For a while, I used to have a nine-to-five job
working in an office as their in-house videographer.
Having a nine-to-five job was extremely time-
consuming but I didn't allow it to eclipse my
real passion. In the evenings after I'd finish work,
I'd go and hit climbs in what I'd been wearing in
the office. I had a foot in both worlds. I'm not one
of those people who thinks everyone should turn
their back on the world. One piece of advice I've
always tried to give to my friends is that it's fine
to be part of the rat race, but don't get caught in
the mouse traps. You can be part of the system,
but always make sure there's something that's
yours, something you love that can't be stripped
from you. Your passions will keep you happy.
Some people manage to turn their passion into
their career, some people have their nine-to-five
job but make time in the evenings and weekends
for what they love.

Often the photos that mean the most to me are
nothing to do with whether the thing was the
highest or the biggest or the most sketchy, it's
about the memories that come with it. When I'm
looking back on my life, I'm going to be able to say
'Those stories, those nights out with my friends,
are priceless.' You can't buy that stuff. The only
way you can make these memories is by getting
out of your comfort zone and making connections
with people. I don't exactly believe in an afterlife

or reincarnation, and I think you have to treat each minute with the value it deserves. I believe this is it, you get one go, one opportunity to give it your all. The only thing I will leave behind is the legacy I've built and the memories I've made with other people. I'll never forget the memories that go along with these photographs. I just wish it wasn't so cheesy on Instagram, with people posting a photo of a sunset with 'Make memories while you can'. The idea is right, but it's just so diluted now.

This was one of the first climbs I ever did. It was for a 4oD video about people climbing buildings called *Urban Explorers.* This was a long time ago.

Some people may have noticed I've broken my three points of contact rule here. In freerunning you have something we call an overgrip. As you can see in the photo, my palm is on top and my fingers are able to wrap behind. This type of grip essentially gives me almost double the hold compared to a standard corner grip.

In love
with the
city

► When you do this sport you inhabit the city more than other people. Most people go through their city in a really limited way, looking to get from one place to another. They take the same commute to work, sitting there cursing at the traffic, never looking up, only at their phones. I swear if you ask most people about their city they would be negative. It's dirty, polluted, grey, covered in pigeon crap and graffiti. But it's like they're taking it for granted. Routine deadens you to things. One of the most valuable things in life is contrast, otherwise it all just blurs into one. If you don't have darkness you don't appreciate light, and when you don't have sadness you won't know happiness.

When you do the stuff that we do, you experience a new perspective on things. You build a bond with the structure that you're climbing, one that most people wouldn't understand. It's based on respect. For us, climbing something isn't disrespectful, but so many people seem to see it in that way. All I can say is that I bet I know more about my city than them, about the architecture, about what it's made of. That's not because I'm some geography geek who was going out with a map and a compass before this, it's because in order to be able to do this, I've had to pay real attention.

Through exploration I've come to realize how beautiful everything is. Now, when I travel about the city I'm subconsciously looking up, thinking about possible routes and climbs, ways that I could use a certain part of the city in a different way.

You also start to look for beauty where other people don't; in an empty half-built room with water on the floor, or in these utility tunnels that run under central London. Me and my good friend Dibs found this manhole that had just been left open and right above it was this big sign that said 'No Cycling', so we couldn't resist getting some Boris bikes and taking them down for a ride. (Obviously we took them back and parked them in their proper place.) They're crazy tunnels. It's another way that you see something different about the city. It's like going backstage at a theatre, it's all the bits they don't want you to see that keep the city working. As much as anything else, it felt pretty gangster to have a private underground bike route all to ourselves.

Don't be ashamed of passion

▶ I would say climbing buildings is a by-product of what I love. The buildings are the challenge, they're the things that require effort and training and dedication, but it's spending time with your friends, it's meeting those challenges, it's that feeling that you all have together, that you can do this, that you've found a way to overcome it. It's those memories that I will have for my whole life.

I think that's why young boys love sport, because it's somewhere you can focus your passion and dedication and talent that's safe. You see grown men crying if they lose a big match and everyone understands, they don't mock it. But if you go and see a film, or listen to a bit of music and cry, that's something to be ashamed of. As someone who dedicates so much of my time to taking risks, people often ask me, 'What are you afraid of?' I get this question a lot and the only legit answer I have is the thought of being 90 years old on my deathbed and looking back at my life with regret. Looking back at a life full of 'what-ifs'. That terrifies me. I live my life as if I've been given the chance of doing it all over again.

That doesn't mean doing anything, there's stuff – some stuff – where the risk doesn't feel worth it. But anyone who's ever done anything has got past the moments when people think they're crazy. You don't change the status quo by doing exactly what everyone else has done. In my tiny way, I hope that the people who respond to these images and my videos are responding to that spirit.

I know that there are going to be people that don't get it, however much you try to communicate it. We're told people are crazy when a lot of the time they're the most sane. I don't understand the idea of settling for a life where you can't live to your maximum potential. I can't understand choosing a life that's the same as one that's been lived millions of times by other people. Don't get me wrong, I know how it happens, I know that there are pressures on people, they need to provide for their family, unexpected things come along, they need to make their family proud and their family might only understand certain kinds of life. But I'm lucky enough to have no one depending on me – for now, I'm making my life the shape I want it to be.

I know so many people my age who seem like they're happy to wait for some sort of life to appear, or to only do the things that aren't hard and risky. Even if you don't succeed at anything you want to do, you know that the ride is going to be worth it. No one ever learns anything about themselves from doing something they already know they can do. If it excites you but scares you, if you take that chance, even if it seems risky, you will get the reward.

Fear

▶ People ask if I'm afraid when I'm on top of a building. The truth is I'm not anymore. I'm cautious. I'm careful. I'm aware of the danger and I respect it. But I don't feel fear. I keep coming back to driving a car – that's two tonnes of metal that you're in control of. It's terrifying if you haven't trained to know how to use it. It's all about control. We're all afraid of stuff. People think I have guts of steel, or that I'm mental. They think it's mad. It's not that I'm not afraid when I look down from the top of a 45-metre building and see the drop.

So many people are so afraid all of the time. Afraid to try, afraid to say they like something, afraid to say they care about something. Especially when you're a young guy.

You have to innovate with whatever you've got. I'm not saying that I don't like chilling with my mates, playing PlayStation 4. It's not like every minute of every day that I'm looking for excellence. But I know that I've found something that I would rather do than anything else.

I don't do it for the subscriber numbers, for the hits and the ad revenue, though those are things that I believe will come if I'm making good videos, photographing good images.

We're all scared of things. Scared of people laughing at us. Scared of not being good at something. Scared of being vulnerable.

Fear is the number-one killer of ambition. Fear of what people will think of you, fear of what could go wrong, fear of being vulnerable. You have to get to the point in your life when you get past the fear. Life is too short to allow your decisions to be shaped by fear.

Respect

▶ Such a big part of climbing is having respect
for what you're going to do. Planning and
knowing what you're going to come up against.
What sort of night it is, the weather, the air
temperature, what sort of a surface you're going
to be climbing on. We know about different types
of granite, different types of concrete, brick,
what sort of grip you need, what it's like to move
on. You become interested in how they make
buildings, how they're put together, but also,
how it looks, what it's for. You get this sense of
the different parts of the buildings. There are bits
of the building you're meant to live or work in,
then places you're meant to just look at, areas
no one ever goes to, and we get to spend time
there. You're seeing behind the scenes of the
building – like being backstage at a show.

Rooftops – Finding My Way

▶▶ But you have to realize that the building is in charge, you can't dominate it or beat it. There's only one winner between the building and you; you have to find the route that's already there, be able to see it. I feel as if that balance of respect and confidence is key in life. If you're genuinely confident, you don't need to make noise, to shout other people down. You've got to be confident and back yourself and know what you're capable of, but ultimately you have to be humble. The environment decides what you do and how you do it.

You constantly have to have it in your mind – is what I'm holding safe? I'm about to put my life in my own hands, is this sturdy, is it rusty, is it fixed to the wall? You can never 100 per cent know until you're on it but you have to constantly be thinking about this stuff, weighing it up. Honestly, the amount of care and attention you have to have – people have this idea that we're these thoughtless risk-takers but I challenge anyone to find people who are thinking as much about their surroundings and measuring what they're capable of against what's happening as us on a climb.

When I'm doing a climb I stay as relaxed as I possibly can. If you let yourself panic, you start making bad decisions. That's where all the practice kicks in. If I had to think about every little thing I was doing, I'd get overwhelmed and start to freeze up. Your brain is capable of so much stuff. It's like when you watch an average fourteen-year-old playing FIFA, they're doing really complex stuff. It's just generally not valued, so people don't give any credit for it. When they start doing brain surgery with PlayStation controllers, suddenly everyone will get it.

Life in the penthouse

▶ It's not complicated when you think about going to high places and why people get annoyed. High places are for rich people. The penthouse is where you put the richest resident; the head of the bank gets the best view. The same apartment on the fiftieth floor is worth much more than on the fifth floor. We know views have a value. One of the things that annoys the people who own the buildings is that we're nobodies gaining access to these views for free. There's a reason they keep the rich up there, in the light, in the fresh air, in all that glass and shiny metal. The only time you really see the underprivileged up high in the city is when they're in tower blocks. You keep the poor depressed, easy to market to, happy to buy stuff, while the rich are up there looking down, ready to make money from you.

I get a lot of people telling me that I'll grow out of this, that it's just a teenage rebellious phase. I definitely accept that I have a difficult relationship with authority. I'm one of those people who thinks that respect should be earned. I don't enjoy being told how to do something, I enjoy exploring it and working out how to do it myself, that's just the sort of person I am. I want to understand why your idea is better than mine.

I don't want to follow, I don't want to spend my life helping someone thirty floors above me in an office achieve their dreams because they were brave enough to chase them. I want to be the one bringing people along with me from the front. My goal is not to follow blindly, my goal is to lead, educate and inspire.

Up
in the
clouds

▶ This was one of the first really tall buildings
I'd ever done. This guy spent about a week,
with a zoom lens, taking shots to try to work out
the best route to the crane and not get stopped.
It almost felt like mission impossible. We finally
plucked up the courage to hit it. Because it's
a privately owned area and all the different
landowners have their own security, there were
just so many guards there.
This is next to Canary Wharf. That's another thing
you find out when you start spending time in that
area of London, it's all called something wharf.
Then you look down and you see the shape of the
docks and where the warehouses would have been
and you think about how that part of the city has
changed from being a place where ships came in;
now it's thousands of people up in the sky, pressing
buttons and trading. The names round there are
incredible – Crossharbour, Mudchute.

►► We managed to get to the crane but soon realized we would have to squeeze through a safety guard. I got through and left my bag to be passed to me. But as I went to take it, I somehow managed to drop the entire thing. The bag fell and landed in the basement, making this insane bang. We were sneaking into somewhere with guards and dogs everywhere, we were supposed to be as quiet as possible, but no one heard.

The red lights on top of cranes are there to stop helicopters and planes from crashing into them. You can see in the previous photo how the light starts to bleed out sideways, and that's because we were so high up we were pretty much at cloud level and the light is shining out across the clouds. I tried to capture it but you can see that it hits the clouds and goes parallel to the horizon.

This next shot is halfway through sunrise. It doesn't look like London, it looks completely different. I can remember sitting up there, it's so relaxing. That's what you realize when you go up there, that all these banks that have their head offices, all of the people making decisions about our money, they're up there, looking down. In some ways you can see how they forget that there are real people down there, living their lives. It all looks so calm, the noise of the city is so distant.

Perspective

▶ I'm not interested in that kind of over-the-top, thrill-chasing extreme stuff. People trying to do the craziest thing, hanging off the edge of a crane by their little finger. It's not about pushing the boundaries just for the sake of it. There's this theory that astronauts have about when you go into space and look down at the earth from a distance. It's called the Overview Effect. When you see the earth high up, so far away, you get this cognitive shift and you see how tiny we really are. You see how small the earth is and it puts all of your concerns and worries into a new perspective. I think this idea resonates with many of the people that climb. We've seen the city from so many different angles, we've seen how it fits together, how messy it can be, that we get a little overview effect of the city. Most people only see their little patch of the city, these huge buildings towering down over them, with lobbies and security guards and receptions, and they feel intimidated, they feel that parts of the city aren't for them to use, to be in. When you rise above the city and see it from so many different angles, you realize how small everything is. I think we're much more interested in how things are connected, what we have in common, rather than what separates us.

▶▶ When you only have a really limited perspective, that's when you start to get really protective of what you do have. When you remove any sense of opportunity, that's when people start getting violent about their territory, their postcode, and will start to act territorial to protect it, because that's what they've got to feel ownership of. I'm sure if you took people involved in gang violence and showed them the city from the perspectives we see it, it would have a positive effect. We spend so much time stressing about things that seem so important. We over-complicate everything and rarely take a moment to step back and see what really matters. Taking risks and living a life filled with uncertainty has given me a new perspective on things. It's allowed me to realize how simple things can be. We're slightly evolved organisms living on a rock flying through space and time. What's the point of doing things that don't make you happy? We should all take more time to appreciate the beauty of the universe.

Outlaws

▶ Many people think we're breaking the law with what we do. It's true that we do often have to run away, usually to stop the aggravation of dealing with private security. The reality is that as long as we aren't vandalizing, stealing or damaging anything to get where we are going then there is no crime. The owners of the building can decide to prosecute us for trespass, but this would lead to a civil prosecution, not criminal.

We never damage anything and we try and respect private security as much as we can. We completely understand that they are just doing their job, living their life, feeding their family.

I have as much of a right to film them on my camera as they do to film me on their CCTV.

I'm not going to lie, there have been some brushes with the authorities that have been pretty scary. Following my particular passion has meant official letters, dealings with the police and a very worried mum after they raided my house for pretty much every electronic item we owned. I only show my audience the incredible views, the fun videos.

But I have to be honest about the consequences too and the impact this has had on people I love. In an ideal world doing what I do wouldn't come with these complications, but in a weird way, it shows me just how strongly I feel about it. Because I'm not going to let it stop me.

I hope whatever anyone else's passion is, they overcome the obstacles in their way.

Believe

► This was one of the first nights I really set out to capture some amazing shots. I'd just bought my first proper DSLR and I was ready to see what I could produce. It was around this time I was first getting into Instagram and social media, realizing how interesting it was being able to catch scenes and views. I began to discover these Instagram photographers whose work really stood out and inspired me. There was one photographer in particular who had a few hundred thousand followers and he became someone I really looked up to. I went out on one of my first nights with my camera and sent him one of the shots I captured. To my surprise, he reposted my photos with the caption: 'Watch out for this kid, he's going to be one of the best.' It was incredible to receive such credit from someone who inspired me so much. At times, no matter how dedicated you are to something, it's still empowering to be told you're on the right track.

Rooftops – Spreading My Wings

Opinions

► When I first started out on this journey, especially on social media, being confident was one of the hardest challenges I had to face. To be totally honest, I was really scared of what people would think of me and scared of what they'd say about me. Especially because it's not like you're an actor or a singer, there's no part or performance to hide behind, it's just you being yourself. Gaining confidence was a slow process of learning how it felt to have people express their opinions of me but what matters most was I learned to deal with those opinions. Especially the negative ones. After a while I came to the realization that I would never allow the negative opinion of a random person I had never met stop me from achieving my goals.

You realize that opinions don't actually exist. They're just neurons going off in someone else's head. The fact that someone thinks you're a dick doesn't mean you are, any more than the number of people who believe the world is 4,000 years old means that it is. Now, that doesn't mean that you can do anything! There are objective things that would make you a dick. But if you post a video of you trying to do something and someone's response is an insult, the only thing you can tell from that is they're probably not the happiest of people. If something makes you happy, do it.

I'd be lying if I said that sometimes you don't get a bit annoyed. You drove five hours through the night to arrive somewhere at sunrise and climb 90 metres up a bit of metal in the rain and then someone comments 'Big whoop' and you're like, 'C'mon, man'. I think the majority of the feedback I receive is pretty positive, probably about 95 per cent, but what's funny is that it's the 5 per cent that motivates me twice as much. So many of the criticisms centre around the idea that we shouldn't be getting attention for what we do, because it's stupid and not worth the risk, but then you look at these guys that climb up cliffs without safety ropes in Yosemite National Park.

Your passion might not be someone else's

▶ I get that for people that have never done it, the risk doesn't feel worth the reward. For people that have never played sport, the idea of crying at losing a game seems silly. Personally, the idea of feeling some sense of connection with millionaire footballers because they happen to play for a team seems a tiny bit absurd to me. But millions of people do. If you don't share a passion, it seems illogical, ridiculous, childish. Some people travel the world to see paintings, or listen to a particular conductor of an orchestra. Some people love opera, others think it's a bunch of fat people screaming. Following your passion means breaking new ground and that's exciting. Just don't expect everyone to get it straight away.

Balfron Tower

▶ We started exploring all these different estates, looking for cool buildings to climb and interesting shots. This building is on a stunning Brutalist estate in Poplar, in East London. They're tearing it down at the moment. We had word that the architect who designed the estate had a flat on the top floor, which is now stripped and abandoned. You can actually see dinosaur and plane stickers on the window. We were pretty sure that this desolate space we were standing in was once a child's room. It's amazing, the idea that in the middle of this abandoned building you can still find these little ghosts of the people that lived there.

It makes you think so much about what a building is for when you see it abandoned, or when you see the parts of a building that you're not meant to see. It's when you remember that buildings are tools, they're for humans to use, to live and work in, to be with other people in. The number of buildings you see as you climb and explore around London that are empty – they just never have anyone in, they're like show homes because they're an investment for someone who's never been there, they don't even have people to stay there. The whole of the centre of the city has been gutted of people; it's just office buildings and apartments with nothing in the fridge.

At least with these buildings, some people say they're ugly but they were built for people, they were thought about as places for people to live in. The council blocks were built to try to get people out of the slums, out of the dirt and into the sky. It didn't work and you can see why when you go round most of them – because they're falling apart, the lifts don't work, the windows are choked up with dirt – but at least they were trying to put normal people up there in the sky. People have started to realize how political this becomes in the aftermath of a tragedy like Grenfell; it's just so sad it's taken something like that for people to begin to have those conversations.

Sometimes you glimpse into windows and you see these whole other worlds. With lots of the office buildings, you can't see into them from outside, but the people inside can see out.

Petticoat Tower

▶ This is a brick-made residential tower in central London. When you stop to think about why roads have their names – Petticoat Lane, Brick Lane – they are from a time when it was a completely different city and people used it in different ways. I live in East London and so many different groups of people have come here – Jewish, Irish, Bengali. You can see when you look down at it, it's this mix of old and new, all these different areas all jumbled together. It's when people have nothing that they get obsessed with keeping their little patch of something free of new people. When you feel happy and confident, when you've got options and choices, you don't mind so much.

A bridge, Stratford

▶ I think this shot really stands out because we managed to capture so many different aspects of the city in one image. The bridge going across, the train moving down the rails towards the station. You can see the Shard in the distance.

It's this area of London that was completely changed by the Olympics. It's a whole new place now, compared to what it was.

I had to run up this bridge with the right grip on my feet, or I'd slide all the way down. We're using a really, really long lens on a tripod, and after I'd set up the framing, I ran round and climbed up the bridge. I had my good friend on speakerphone, on my phone in my pocket. As I saw a train, I counted down and we managed to capture everything happening at once.

What I like is that we see the city in a more joined-up way. Most people maybe know one or two bits well, or they might know how to walk around central London, but for most of us it's the tube and train map or bus routes that let us know how things fit together. When you're up high, you see that the city isn't really this separated thing but it's all one, all joined up. London Bridge and Stratford are separate places but because I've explored every single vein and artery of the city, I feel like I have a much closer relationship with it. I have much more of a sense of how far apart things are.

London is so awkward in the way it's been set out. It's not a planned city, with numbered streets as you go up, like New York with its blocks and straight lines. It's just built up with layers of different stuff all growing around itself. It's like when you see a tree growing next to a railing in a park and it kind of just grows into it and around it. That's why I love it so much. When you're up high, you have this old nineteenth-century building and then behind it a modern glass-fronted building and it just means you have all these angles. I like the idea that a city isn't planned – it's not a thing that you just plug people into, it's there to grow and change as people need different things from it. That's what I think we're part of, that spirit of making the city what you want it to be, not passively using it as this tiny group of rich people want you to. It's a way more complicated city to understand, but that's why it's so rewarding. You can't love something if it's too cold and neat.

Residential building, Elephant and Castle

► Often when you're out early in the morning around these big buildings in the city, it's dead. There are cleaners but nobody really lives there and the offices are mostly empty. But in Elephant and Castle, we had to try this twice because it turned out Ministry of Sound was holding a student event literally next to the access point for the climb and there were hundreds of people queued up opposite where we were supposed to be sneaking into. We had to come back another day.

It's funny to come face to face with the contrasting lives people choose to live. Two types of people the same age. Them queuing up to an event to get drunk and listen to music, us trying to sneak up onto a roof to see an incredible view. All of us with the intention of experiencing something that makes us feel alive.

Rooftops – Spreading My Wings

Barbican Estate

▶ During summer 2017, we hadn't really hit many things. We were good at photography but we hadn't really hit any of the tallest structures and there were people in the scene who were teasing us on social media, telling us to go do something good. So we accepted the challenge and in one six-week period we hit pretty much every big location they'd ever done.

I like that this is an old building that got run down but they didn't tear it down and start again, they refurbished it. People call it ugly but I think it's amazing. It's that Brutalist, concrete feeling, like the Southbank.

The Barbican Estate is one of the most beautiful in London in my opinion. It's amazing for freerunning and has so much potential for different routes and runs. I've spent so many hours there I've come to build a relationship with it. My mum hates it; we were driving past it once and my mum said, 'Look how ugly that building is.' My only reaction was 'I can't believe you said that.'

People think these buildings are eyesores but I think they're amazing.

There's a lot of stuff aimed at stopping people using buildings and space from the way they were expressly designed. So there are benches that homeless people can't lie down on, or even spikes on surfaces where they might be able to, rails to stop people riding bikes or to stop skaters, certain sorts of plants with thorns to stop people going off the path. It's called hostile architecture. With freerunning, it's really hard to actually stop people because the barriers become something you can work into your route. They can put up anti-climb paint and spikes but they tend to make the area look really ugly and unfriendly, so they don't usually go all out with them. Security is a massive one; they move you on or away from buildings. The people I run with always try to be respectful with security guards. If we do get kicked off a spot, you have to be respectful, not protest or try to make aggro. The thing is, part of the sense of satisfaction probably does come from the planning, how you're going to make sure you don't get caught by security.

It's fun going up these sorts of buildings but we knew we needed to start hitting some of the really tall ones. So we started exploring the city.

The City within the city

► If you're looking for tall buildings to climb, you end up spending lots of time in certain parts of the city. There's Docklands, obviously, but there's also the proper City – Bank, Liverpool Street and that whole area. As you climb through London you see so many buildings leaving their lights on through the whole night. You're taught that if you leave a room you should turn the lights off. The only people there for most of the night are the cleaners for a few hours. So why are the lights on for the rest of the time? They are there to be looked at and admired, they are part of the story that a city is telling about itself: it's open for business all night, it's the sort of city that has skyscrapers. And that's what people find difficult, I think, because part of that story is that you admire the skyscrapers and look at them from below and by extension you admire the building, what the building seems to represent about the company.

We used to build cathedrals for people to look up at and now we build skyscrapers for investment banks. You stay down there and let the people that sit up there in all that light and glass invest your money and don't question them. But what we do is get up where they are and that seems like a lack of respect to some people. But I think people should examine what exactly we should be respecting. I am the most understanding of someone making a living, feeding their family, doing a job, but I just want people to think about why you should challenge certain things. Even if you don't get out there physically, think about why they might not want you to. No one ever did anything great by doing exactly what they were told. There's nothing more frustrating than not being able to be who you are. That doesn't matter if you're designing iPhones or working in a supermarket, trust me. Bring yourself to work, school, college, don't be afraid to be yourself.

Rebels

▶ What I find interesting is that a lot of the people who are now in positions of power most likely had the same mindset as us at some point in their lives. Living through the punk and hippie eras – the idea of being yourself, upsetting the order – they must recognize that. I think at some point people will look at what we're doing and see it as true art. People are waking up to the fact that we have time to do all this because we're not sitting there watching reality TV. For fifty years you had this box and you knew people would be in front of it at a certain time and you showed them adverts. You had newspapers that pretty much everyone read at least one of, so you showed them adverts. Now for our generation you don't have that, you have people making their own videos and sending them to their friends, all at the same time, whenever they want to, or Snapchatting, and these companies are still trying to find ways of selling things. Don't get me wrong, I love people purchasing my posters and clothing and sending me pictures of them wearing it. It makes me feel amazing that I have people willing to support what I do. It feels incredible to have a business built out of something I love.

But if I ever felt like it was business first and I'd lost the passion, I'd move on. I know there are people out there in the world doing madder stuff, climbing higher buildings, taking bigger risks. If I started getting into that arms race, I wouldn't be able to compete with someone who is willing to risk everything. I can only do what I do, continuing to create images and videos that I think are beautiful and exciting. If I've opened my followers' eyes to the idea that there are bigger horizons, if I've got a few people to look up from their phones and look at the skyline, or just go outside and think about getting in better shape, I'm happy. I want people to look at my images and videos and feel something.

London Stadium

▶ Everything about the West Ham video was mad. At every point we just expected to get stopped, but there was the wedged-open door, then an unlocked security gate. Still we thought we'd get stopped. But we got out to the pitch, sat in the manager's seat. We must have been seen on a hundred cameras, but no one came and stopped us. I remember the sheer amount of light from the floodlights. A lot of people thought my West Ham video was fake because the lights were on. The West Ham stadium video was the one that went really big. Compared to lots of videos it was pretty easy. Many people were upset and

alarmed about how easy it was for us to gain access. We set out assuming that we wouldn't be able to get in. As we climbed in they were making it the West Ham stadium, after the Olympics. We realized that there were hundreds of cameras but no one was watching them. We were so annoyed we hadn't brought a football. That video has been watched by six million people and went on the news. Everyone made a big deal out of the security.

At the time my most-viewed video had 20,000. I uploaded the West Ham video before I met some mates and when I looked at my phone later there were 100,000 views.

My family weren't that fussed. We'd had a lot of arguments about me climbing and exploring. Me and my mum weren't actually talking at the time because she was so keen on me getting a proper job and I refused. We hadn't spoken the whole day and I said, 'I've gone viral', which she didn't know as an expression, so she was probably even more worried. It took a few days and she realized what I'd been working on. I completely understand why she'd feel like that.

Six months before the West Ham video, I was doing furniture delivery. I was always good at delivering to the top floors. I think there's this idea that everyone always believes in people right from the beginning, and maybe that's true if you're from certain backgrounds, but my mum, completely understandably, was like, 'There's a reason the careers advisers don't have jumping about on buildings as a job.' But I think if you live your life by what other people think are the limits of what you'll achieve, you'll never find anything out. No one who ever did anything good did it by just doing exactly what other people have done. You have to learn from other people, build on what they've done, but there has to be the moment when you take it that bit beyond.

Are you going to do something respectable, or something interesting?

The
Sidemen
Tower

There's a whole generation of people with jobs that their parents' generation can't begin to understand. That doesn't mean everyone can be a makeup blogger, but we need to realize that the next thing like that will feel just as absurd to the previous generation. Technology is changing how we relate to everything. I understand why my parents and teachers and other people look at what I do and don't understand how it can be a valid choice as to how I spend my time. Just like they can't understand how filming yourself playing videogames with your mates or doing makeup tutorials can be a job. But it's the same stuff people always want – they want to feel inspired, they want to feel like someone understands them and their life, that they're not alone. I want to inspire people, so that when they get told that their passion isn't real, or doesn't count, they know that they can make up their own life. What I love about posting videos is that it doesn't demand that you went to the right school or the right university. People respond to your passion, to you – it's a really honest relationship with your followers. If you start by trying to sell them something, they can sniff it out, you need to genuinely give them something of yourself.

► After the West Ham video, things were crazy for a while. We decided to do another big one and ended up climbing the Sidemen Tower. This was a dangerous one. It's pretty much a ladder to the top. A very high ladder. I've been doing this for almost ten years. I have spent countless hours outside and in gyms training on bars and doing muscle ups and laches. I trust my body completely. I chalk my hands. I'm in my element. I have the three points of contact rule: either two hands one foot, or two feet one hand. I just stay completely calm, have fun with it, and don't make rash decisions. If I don't have a GoPro on me, I have to use one hand to climb. For the Sidemen Tower I had a GoPro in my mouth. You're not thinking about how high you are, you're thinking about the next move, to be safe. We did another video at a Sidemen event, too, doing a flip over the edge of a shopping centre. They've been really supportive and they get what I'm trying to do with my content.

Humber Bridge

▶ My friend Ryan Taylor and I were looking for the next crazy thing to attempt. He's a professional BMX rider and YouTuber. Also a person with the same adventurous mindset as me. We were searching for the tallest structures in the country and found the Humber Bridge. The tallest bridge in the UK.

It was a five-hour drive from London to Hull; we left at around 11 p.m. that night and arrived for sunrise. It was tricky to find a parking spot so by the time we actually left the car and made our way to the bridge, the sun was already up. It's a suspension bridge so we used the massive cables to our advantage. We jumped up and literally walked up 155 metres to the very tip. The circular cables were moist with morning dew and freezing. The higher you walk the steeper it gets. The fatigue in your legs becomes more intense with every single step. The uncertainty of whether the cars below can see you or whether the police are already on their way sticks in the back of your mind. Regardless of these uncertainties, the moment we reached the tip they completely faded. I was filled with a feeling of excitement and awe. The sunrise views were breathtaking 155 metres above the Humber river, and on each side you can see patchwork fields that lead off into the distance.

After around thirty minutes we realized the security cameras had started spinning and facing towards us; this was the moment we knew we had to leave, and quickly. We ended up pretty much running down the cable. When you're faced with this situation it's kind of like you enter a zone where your hand–eye coordination becomes sharper and the decisions you make become instinct. You see every obstacle, every bolt, every aspect of the metal and potential dangers. It's this really private thing between you and what you're climbing.

One Canada Square

► One Canada Square: a building with such status and prestige that not once in my life did I think that I would one day sit on the very tip. It's the second tallest building in the UK. You can see it wherever you are in London. I've spent my entire life travelling around it, so it's completely familiar to me. Again, we went in expecting it to be impossible but managed to pull off something that would go down in history in the scene. It really was absurd, sneaking past the concierge into a lift, then into a fire exit and right through every unlocked door straight to the rooftop. From there it was just a short ladder climb up to the inside of the pyramid. That famous flashing light that can be seen from every corner of the city – I was now sitting next to it. The wind was so strong we could barely hear each other speak. It was almost impossible to get a semi-decent shot. The memory of what it felt like when that last door was opened and I knew it was going to be possible is one that will stay with me till the day I die.

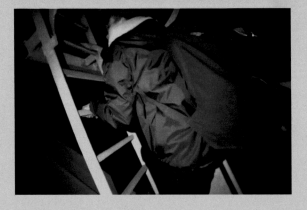

Skyscrapers

Seeing the World

Jakarta

Santorini

Make it challenging

Dubai

Shanghai

Jakarta

► One of the most amazing things that's happened since the West Ham stadium video has been that people have started inviting me to climb all around the world. All I've ever wanted is to see as much as I can, to experience as much as possible. So to be able to do that because of my passion is incredible.

This is the Wonderful Indonesia headquarters, the Ministry for Tourism. They gave us permission to go up on the roof. It's so interesting how different their attitudes were.

We were taken out there by the Ministry as an influencer trip. The place couldn't be more different to London. I went to an ancient village where they were having a traditional festival and I asked if I could take some footage with a drone and they were like 'Of course!' It's crazy to me now that I can get taken around the world by someone because they want me to show the buildings to my followers.

Santorini

▶ Santorini in Greece is just this incredible
place for freerunning and climbing. It's like if a
freerunner died and went to heaven, this is what
it would be. There are all these white houses
up in the hills that make it look like a film set.
I knew I wanted to do a link in my video where
I jumped into this pool on the roof of one of the
buildings and edit to landing in the sea. So I found
this water to jump into on one of the rooftops but
didn't think that would mean I was walking around
dripping wet for the rest of the day. We got some
amazing footage with a drone up on the mountain,
which is where this picture was taken.

Make it challenging

► All of these images were taken from one incredible night in LA. I was in Vegas for a project that my friend had asked if I wanted to be involved in where this guy wanted to spray-paint his entire mansion. After around ten days of being in this house I decided that I needed to get out and explore. I had met these girls there who told me they were going on a road trip to LA and asked if I wanted to join. Of course I said yes! After a few days in LA the girls went back to Vegas and I stayed in LA. I was on a mission to explore as much as possible and get as many shots as I could.

There was one specific day I remember where I had just finished a climb with this kid I met and he had to leave to go help his mother. I was alone in the middle of downtown LA, I knew nobody and it was just me, myself and my camera. I remember saying to myself, 'No, I'm not going to let this day go to waste – I am going to find something to do no matter what.' After a while I stumbled across one of the tallest buildings and asked one of the security if there was a viewing platform on the top. Turns out there was and it was free. At the top I bumped into this street photographer who was also out shooting. We got talking and I said I wanted to hit some rooftops. He called up his friend who was a rooftopper and said, 'Yo, I'm with this guy from England who wants to hit some rooftops – can you let us know of any that we can try?' And the first thing this guy says on the phone is, 'Are you with Nightscape?!' He'd seen on my Instagram story that I was in LA and sent through a list of potential rooftops.

From there we tried a few and just happened to be attempting one at the exact same time as two other rooftoppers. Me and these other rooftoppers got talking and they asked if I wanted to cruise around LA with them and see what rooftops we could hit. That night we ended up hitting about six rooftops in total and I made some new friends.

I could have just gone back to my Airbnb because I felt a bit scared or intimidated, but instead I opened myself up, took a risk and ended having one of the best nights of my life. That's why I believe it's so important to get out of your comfort zone. You never know where it will take you and what you will learn.

Dubai

▶ Dubai just has this crazy thing for skyscrapers, man. It's like they just turn it up to eleven. People ask you if it gets scarier the higher you go. It's definitely got an extra kick at 70 storeys, but the whole point is that, even then, you've drilled this stuff so much, you know your skills so well, that if you can do it at 10 feet you can do it at 310 feet. The only difference is your mental approach, so you just have to learn to conquer that.

At night, you'd look down and see these massive freeways, built for ten times as many cars as they have now, all lit up in orange and blue, like you're in a science-fiction film. Everyone there was so friendly, though, so up for us showing off their city to the world.

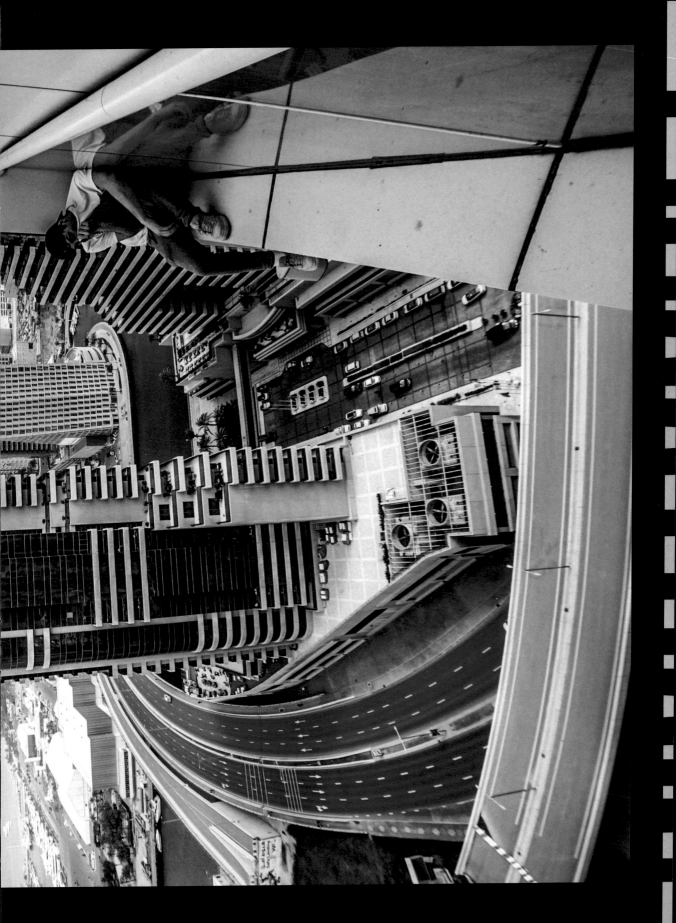

Shanghai

▶ There are 35 million people in Shanghai, so they have this need for skyscrapers to fit everyone in. The density of people and buildings is just amazing. When you're up there looking down it looks like an alien planet. Shanghai is incredible. So many massive buildings, so much building work all the time. Honestly, it can be midnight and there are these showers of sparks raining down as they're welding.

I think back to when I was starting out, making videos of us climbing in our local estates, or before that, when I was a twelve-year-old, hanging out next to the IMAX in Waterloo. You have that fear, of trying to do something, of getting it wrong and these older kids laughing at you. But they don't. It's this community where you're encouraged to try, where you help each other, support each other. And that's what I'll take with me. That fear is there for a reason, but it can be conquered. Without fear, without risk, you're not doing it right. It's when we feel fear but go beyond it that we really live.

Behind the Scenes

Kit

Editing

What's next?

01 **Notepad**
02 **DJI Mavick Pro drone**
03 **House keys**
04 **Sigma 24mm lens f/ 1.4**
05 **Canon 50mm f/ 1.8 STM**
06 **GoPro Hero Session**
07 **Sony a7SII**
08 **Samyang 14mm f/ 2.8**
09 **Bic Cristal (black)**
10 **MacBook Pro**
11 **Mavick RC**
12 **Coloured smoke grenades**
13 **Rubik's cube (unsolved)**
14 **Nightscape SD baggie**
15 **Miscellaneous SDs**
16 **Nishika N8000 35mm Quadrascopic Stereo 3D film camera**
17 **Mavick batteries**
18 **Sony batteries**
19 **Lacie Mini Drives**

Editing

► I edit the videos to music, so that the movement is on the beat. I'm making the video dance with the music. It's like how a dancer moves to hit the beat with each movement, so I'm editing in the same way. About 90 per cent of my cuts are on a beat.

I taught myself to edit from scratch. As I said, I had a job as a videographer for a photography company at first. I'd leave work, go climb my buildings and then go home. I decided that my whole life was about climbing but I had no time to do it because of the job, so I chose to concentrate on doing the thing I felt passionate about and stop doing the thing I didn't. My family thought I was mad because their view, which I completely understood, was that I had a job, which I was learning stuff from and where I could begin a career. And I was saying no to that so that I could go and jump around buildings.

What's next?

▶ People ask me what's next, if I have a bucket list of things I want to do. There are definitely things I want to try. Places I want to go. I want to climb mountains, see every city in the world. I want to find new ways of trying to take people where I go, to show them the world through my eyes. But I try not to be too specific because the whole point is, if I'm doing it right, I won't be able to guess what's coming next. The only thing I hope is that I'll be proud of who I become. In the same way that if that little boy in the Spiderman pyjamas met me, I think he'd think I was living a pretty good life. I want whoever I turn into in the future to be someone I'd be proud of now.

I know that if I keep working hard, keep putting myself out there, keep pushing what I'm capable of, opening myself up to things, giving myself the chances to be lucky, then I'll be OK.

Behind the Scenes

LIKE
COMMENT
SUBSCRIBE